The aim of the *Earth Quest* series is to examine and explain how shamanic principles can be applied in the journey towards self-discovery – and beyond.

Each person's Earth quest is the search for meaning and purpose in their life – it is the establishment of identity and the realization of inner potentials and individual responsibility.

Each book in the series examines aspects of a life science that is in harmony with the Earth and shows how each person can attune themselves to nature. Each book imparts knowledge of the Craft of Life.

Other Books in the *Earth Quest* Series

BEAUTIFUL PAINTED ARROW
Stories and Teachings from the Native American Tradition
Joseph E. Rael

THE CELTIC SHAMAN
A Handbook
John Matthews

THE DRUID WAY
Philip Carr-Gomm

EARTH LIGHT
The Ancient Path to Transformation
Rediscovering the Wisdom of Celtic and Faery Lore
R.J. Stewart

EARTH MEDICINE
A Shamanic Way to Self Discovery
Kenneth Meadows

LETTERS FROM A WILD STATE
An Aboriginal Perspective
James G. Cowan

THE MEDICINE WAY
A Shamanic Path to Self Mastery
Kenneth Meadows

POWER WITHIN THE LAND
The Roots of Celtic and Underworld Traditions
Awakening the Sleepers and Regenerating the Earth
R.J. Stewart

SHAMANIC EXPERIENCE
A Practical Guide to Contemporary Shamanism
Kenneth Meadows

Tracks of Dancing Light

Joseph E. Rael is an internationally respected visionary, shaman and master story-teller of the Ute and Pueblo Indian traditions. His work includes the use of sound chambers. He is also the author of the best-selling *Beautiful Painted Arrow*.

Lindsay Sutton was born in Manchester and for ten years taught in Yorkshire. She now lives on a croft in Scotland with her family. She works with The Radiance Technique and helps people on their path to personal development and growth using the wisdom of her acquired knowledge.

EARTH QUEST

Tracks of Dancing Light

A NATIVE AMERICAN APPROACH TO UNDERSTANDING YOUR NAME

Joseph E. Rael
(Beautiful Painted Arrow)

and

Lindsay Sutton

ELEMENT

Shaftesbury, Dorset ● Rockport, Massachusetts
Brisbane, Queensland

© Joseph E. Rael and Lindsay Sutton 1993

Published in Great Britain in 1993 by
Element Books Limited
Longmead, Shaftesbury, Dorset

Published in the USA in 1993 by
Element, Inc.
42 Broadway, Rockport, MA 01966

Published in Australia in 1993 by
Element Books Limited for
Jacaranda Wiley Limited
33 Park Road, Milton, Brisbane, 4064

Photograph of Lindsay Sutton Courtesy David Sim, Golspie
Cover design by Max Fairbrother
Design by Roger Lightfoot
Typeset by Footnote Graphics, Warminster, Wilts
Printed and bound in Great Britain by
Redwood Books, Trowbridge, Wiltshire

British Library Cataloguing in Publication
data available

Library of Congress Cataloging in Publication
data available

ISBN 1-85230-434-0

Contents

We came from the Light
And to the Light do we return
For that ultimately is our Destiny

Joseph E. Rael
(Beautiful Painted Arrow)

Acknowledgements

I WOULD LIKE TO THANK the Picuris Pueblo people and the Southern Ute for giving me my birthright that I might be given the opportunity to become a Human, and to thank them too for teaching that to stay in high states of awe for life is the key to sacred living. And mostly for the teaching that it is life's years that cook us through metaphor alongside our personal experiences until such time as we become more and more well done by it and we become more perfectly cooked.

And finally I ask that Waa-Maa-Chi brings great loving blessings to the two Tribes that brought me into the potential possibilities and into the course work of my life.

Joseph, Beautiful Painted Arrow

In the five years of this lifetime that I have known Joseph, Beautiful Painted Arrow, he has helped me to turn my life around so that I am now able to write this book and in my own way help in working towards a more peaceful planet for us all. Joseph has shown me how to apply the lesson of metaphor to every aspect of daily life, thereby raising my different levels of awareness so that I can now touch the deeper significances of all aspects of life, for both myself and others. I hope those of you who read this book will be able to share that awareness.

At this point I would also like to say that the Radiance Technique has supported me throughout. And I would like to thank my dear Judith for keeping my nose to the grindstone.

And I would like to thank Joseph for thanking me for being born.

Lindsay, Tracks of Dancing Light

Preface

I TEACH IN MY LECTURES and seminars how the combination of essences found in ideas came together to formulate the main ideas and how they (the individual essences in every single idea that we hold to be our truth) most often are truths that are reflected in our values and in our attitudes.

I . . . *awareness*
D . . . *doing, action of doing, creativity*
E . . . *placement, reflection*
A . . . *purity, purification, washing*

To explain this further, the letter I sound, signifying awareness, means, 'that which is alive with knowingness'. The letter D sound means 'to suggest the motion or movement of doing something'. The letter sound of E means, 'that which sits in a relationship with the all', and the letter A sound means 'purifying'.

Now let us go back to the start of this discussion. When we combine the letter sounds (vibrations) of the word I-D-E-A our neuromuscular (brain) body is getting the following impulses: that which is alive with knowingness (1) demands that an action be taken (2) and (3) with that which purifies. And because the idea appears as an insight or flash of light it produces a momentary shot of inspired beauty which in turn generates new life in the brain and body cells and the values in the psyche of the individual's experience are enhanced.

In some ways what I am trying to explain is simple, but in some ways it is not.

The next step I teach is for people to make a song of the vowel sounds. In this example (the word 'idea'), these sounds are;

i . . . *eeee*
e . . . *eh*
a . . . *aah*

These sounds should be chanted repeatedly while allowing the physical body and the brain to open up to the knowledge of what is to be done for the 'idea' ceremony dance. The vibrations created by the chanting of the vowels will bring forth the images of what the 'idea' ceremony dance is to look like and as soon as the dance form appears I record it and then I practise it and when I have perfected it I present it to the public.

I do not perform typical Native American ceremony; all the ceremonies that I teach come from my half dreams/ half visions or from my medicine dreams or visions that I get doing my drum dances or other ceremonies that come to me in my visions. Anyone who wants to know me will understand what I am saying here in this statement because:

> To those who believe, no explanation is necessary; to those who do not believe, no explanation is possible.
>
> from the movie *Saint Bernadette*

I teach people by dancing back in time to a time before culture, to that place in universal consciousness before prehistoric societies (American Indian cultures included) received or were given their religious beliefs. The ceremonies that I am teaching have never been done before on the planet in the precise way that I am doing them and I value keeping a direct line to the source of beauty where all that the spirit of beauty wants to do is love us awake.

This is what I think and it is my right as a planetary citizen to be a free soul to love God in my personal ceremonial ways that I share with people at this time on the planet.

Beautiful Painted Arrow

Introduction

WHAT IS THE BASIS for this book? It is a conceptual tool that will help people find patterns and order in their lives which may contain a lot of complexity and confusion. This book is about how, by understanding the essence of one's name, one can begin to realize that underneath the materialistic universe there are recognizable patterns and an order that is spiritual.

Underlying the world of chance is the world of constants that never changes because the breath is the source of life, the constant in the metaphor of life and it never changes but remains constant while the world of chance is the matter materializing life's goals and objectives. The motion of movement is based upon the choices that we make which are always in a state of becoming but never actually become because our perceptions are always changing. The constant of life is the lifegiving breath of the external self manifesting.

The Divine Breath of life inspires matter to create. Through insights it inspires the birthing and nurturing of inner meaning which then inspires matter to materialize the insights into inner knowing. This manifests into the perceptual realities that are always changing into higher realization and understanding.

The vowels in a name are the constants which never

1

become but are always trying to become, whereas the consonants of the name are the constants that always are.

In the same way that numerology can be used as a guide to the greater scheme of things, so too can the sounds made in language, especially the vowel sounds:

A ...*aah* ... means *purification*
E ...*eh*   ... means *placement*
I ...*eeee* ... means *awareness*
O ...*oh* ... means *childlike innocence*
U ...*oo* ... means *carrying*

To understand how this works let us look at Judith, in whom the power of deep healing began when she was told about the meaning of her name. 'Judith' means 'the eyes that see the carrying of creativity in awareness of time up God's stepladder to beyond the beyond'. The main aspects of 'Judith' are carrying and awareness. 'When you gave me the meaning of my name, it was the beginning of me finding my confidence in being who I am.'

How our names are pronounced or sounded is important in gaining a deeper understanding of who we are because sound gives meaning to our qualitative forms.

A name has a hidden inner essence and an outer aspect, both of which flow from the same source and are the doorways for the expression of the person who carries the name, because the hidden inner meaning or essence of a name tells of the person's innate gifts while the outer aspect gives the personal name he or she is to be known by.

The basis of this book is to get people to sing to each other so that we can feel the soothing power of healing that comes when we can feel right back to where we really come from and why we are here. A study of the vowels in your name will show you this. Maybe if you have the vowel 'A' in your name, you are always trying to perfect and purify things. If you have 'E', your emphasis will be on where you are placed on the wheel of life. With 'I', you will be spending a lot of time trying to figure it all out. With 'O' you may be very sensitive and therefore easily hurt, and with 'U', you will want to carry people or things in your life.

Whatever the sounds, they are there to keep you moving and growing in this reality.

Each of us from birth is 'baby' for a while, which means we are in the space of being the sacred path to awareness and purification, and we relate to 'Mum' who is bringing us forth and carrying us, and 'Dad' who created us in purity.

1 The Breath of Creation

THE BREATH (SPIRIT) IDENTIFIES a person by their given name because the breath is the metaphor for the infinite self, the no form place which is in actuality creating materialism through the movements of the persona carrying the name. Consequently life is made up of Breath, Materialism and Movement.

The breath is the constant flow of the lifegiving sustenance that gives identity and support to the spirit force energies that can be awakened in the person's name by singing them, dancing them and by using them. The breath is materializing the insights, revelations or visions that appear from the infinite vastness. These are the connections to the eternal vastness of the eternal self that when articulated properly can be utilized for a greater wholeness in the person.

The breath is the inspiration that induces matter to materialize the multiple dimension of the stream of consciousness through the motion of movement. Consequently the flow of vowel sounds in a name are the connections to the soul whereas the consonants are connections to the eternal vastness of the self in which the soul can grow. The breath is the life of the lungs of the person and so it enlivens the person's will with the vitality necessary for the person to carry their self into themes of heightened awareness and creativity.

The name of the person is the first key we have of his or her spiritual gifts inherited in this life; for example:

JOSEPH: vowel sounds O and E
O . . . *childlike innocence*
E . . . *placement*

Secondly in the process of materialization we look at the historical meaning of the name; for example:

JOSEPH: son of Jacob, from the Hebrew meaning 'he shall add'. Genesis 30:24.

The impact of the socioeconomic and political world systems have an effect on the person's physical lifestyle as well because we come to life's classroom to learn various things and five of these goals are Purity, Placement, Awareness, Innocence and the art of Carrying.

Movement is the constant in the breath's materialization because without it no changes in growth can take place. In the Native American language Tiwa, the word Waa-Maa-Chi is breath, materialism and movement. It is also the word for God.

God is the all-carrying essence so that when God created everything he breathed all of the living ideas into matter and moved them by carrying them into being.

In the beginning, God was his breath, the essence of the 'All in Everything', and then when he looked to see what he had created, he saw that his perception of things created was creating changes that would arise and fall, appear and disappear, because he realized that he was creating within circles that kept appearing and disappearing. Therefore the beingness of observation created the motion of movement – by the very act of observing he was changing what he was seeing and thus creating the art of becoming.

God was the circle of light where the 'All in Everything'

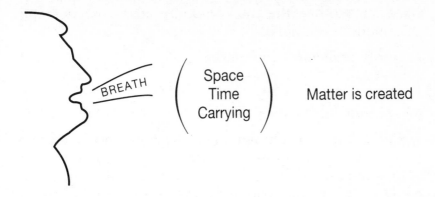

BREATH

(Space
Time
Carrying)

Matter is created

was being created. He breathed in and created the cos-
mos; he breathed out space and time, the body of forms
made of materialism, out of his own beingness. Space
became all the universal bodies, forms and straightness of
direction and time created the movement of goodness,
hence space and time are carried in the Breath Vibration,
Materialism and Movement of all of cosmic thought.

We came from music. Music created all things, it was
from the music that people happened. People were the
vibration of all the ideas that created the two-leggeds, the
four-leggeds, the wingeds and all the creatures of all the
eternities.

And in the beginning there was only Divine longing,
which is the relationship between the lover and the beloved.
We are all longing to make that connection back to the breath
of Great Spirit and it is through the metaphor of sound that
we are able to make that connection to the eternal now.

The lover and the beloved fell into each other's arms
and in their loving sacred dance, they became the reflections, radiances of fusing purity.

And then they crystallized
meaningful moments
into the connections
for all of the eternities.

And then in the sacredness of materialization they became our mother, the Land, and our father, the Sky, and their dance became

of purity and time of radiating
connections of rare awareness
cloaked in the pure shadows of
all spiritual and natural law.

For they knew and understood that they had created in their movements of the sacred dance of creation the inner planes of personal beauty and in time the people would come to enjoy the beautiful metaphoric forms made of experiences alongside ecstasy.

Our ancient ancestors knew that sound was not intended for communication but to enable us to get in touch with the very essence of truth, the sounds of the words were essence connectors and the stories of the ancient storytellers were not only entertaining for the people but had deeper levels of teaching than even the moral teaching. There was a deep resonance in the sounds of all the words.

To become truth that is alive is to be the resonance that flows from the streams of consciousness. We are all the eternities harmonizing and the planet evolves as we evolve. These energies of evolution are in the children's stories of all the traditions of the people who came in the beginning to explain to us that we are metaphor alongside experience.

We are five things and have five things to move through. The five things are Unity and diversity
Struggle
Reconciliation
Purpose
Transformation of potential.

These five things are the five parts of the medicine wheel that we are all here to represent.

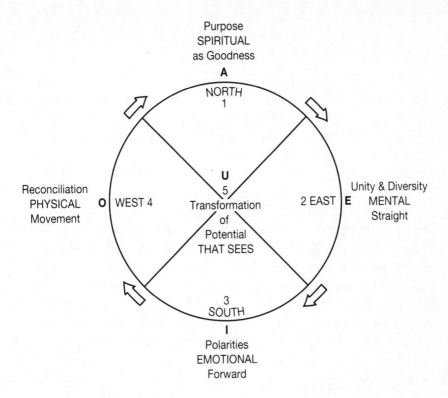

Purpose
SPIRITUAL
as Goodness

Reconciliation
PHYSICAL
Movement

Unity & Diversity
MENTAL
Straight

Polarities
EMOTIONAL
Forward

THE MEDICINE WHEEL

The circle, as in the medicine wheel, is the seed idea because it expresses body weight (gravity), space (gives direction), time (the action of motion).

The circle is the ingredient in life that mandates that we climb up to the breath of the Spirit of Divine Law because the breath's purpose is to purify what is created and so, because this is its function, this is what it does.

Body weight can be physical or it can be the weight we put on a value.

Space gives us the placement we need toward a given direction, while

Time provides the motion as movement that germinates emptiness into manifested materialism.

The space inside the circle gives the direction to each given moment, while the cycles of motion inside the space of the circle create the gravitational body weight needed for motion to materialize our thoughts. Systems created in the space cycles collapse and are not longlasting because they are constantly being interwoven into the tapestry designed to create linear and non-linear time.

Time, in addition to creating the movement required for materialization, also gives us the capacity of perception. Perception creates the impermanence we see in life. The impermanence of life is the fundamental quality that is the basis for the creation of goodness that sets forth the tracks for space to travel its direction. All of the above combinations lead to life's level of integrity. Integrity is a combination of the constant of parts that regulate life's behavioural patterns, and they are:

English language vowels: A E I O U
Five steps of consciousness: 1 2 3 4 5

A – 1. *Straight* – unity and diversity – purity
E – 2. *Forward* – polarities – placement
I – 3. *Movement* – reconciliation – awareness
O – 4. *As goodness* – purpose for our spiritual path – childlike
     innocence
U – 5. *That sees* – transformational potential carrying

The medicine wheel (the seed of life) is:

a mental design   – East
an emotional design – South
a physical design   – West
a spiritual design   – North

created to help us to detach and leap out of the metaphors that existence gives to us inside the medicine wheel.

Where then do we go, having explored and exploited the systems inside the circle of light (the medicine wheel)? We become the essence of the greater whole of life. The circle of life is a hole, made of completion or perfection, originally made to perceive the vastness of the finite and infinite of God's empirical (logical) and universal (intuitive) being.

2   The Vibration of Life

THE VIBRATION IN LIFE is the breath and materializations of our goals and objectives through the direction of movement that we give them. It is through sound vibration that we can connect back to the essence of where we originated from, because it is through our language of verbal and non-verbal communication sounds that we become what we become. It is through the sound vibrations that we create our daily or future realities.

The five vowel sounds of the English language carry the qualities around which our whole way of life out of breath materialism and movement becomes.

A . . . *aah* . . . is *purification*
E . . . *eh* . . . is *placement*
I . . . *eee* . . . is *awareness*
O . . . *oh* . . . is *innocence*
U . . . *ooo* . . . is *carrying*

The five vowels are metaphorically the five fingers on the hand of God and the metaphor meanings of these letters when applied to words which we use give us the key to understanding the very essence of the deep mystery contained within that word.

The consonants too have their own metaphoric meaning and so we can take any consonant in a name and by applying its metaphor meaning we can get down to the original and deepest meaning of the consonant and its connection to the other letters in a name.

THE MEANINGS OF THE FIVE VOWEL SOUNDS OF THE ENGLISH LANGUAGE

A   washing, purity, purification, purifying light
E   reflection, reflectivity, relationship, placing, place-ment, grid, mirror, echo
I   awareness
O   innocence, childlike innocence, circle of light, hollow bone, hollow reed, medicine wheel
U   to carry, carrying light

THE MEANING OF THE CONSONANTS OF THE ENGLISH LANGUAGE

B   path, straight, sacred path
C   beauty, beautify
D   doing, creating, creation, throwing light
F   faith
G   goodness, God
H   stepladder to the heavenly planes, beyond the beyond
J   sight, seeing, vision
K   planting, planting field, (sowing)
L   ascending light
M   to bring forth, manifesting, matter
N   the personal and infinite self
P   heart, centre, sunset
Q   initiation, eternal quest
R   radiance, radiating light, abundance
S   one half of eternity
T   time, crystallized light, speeding light that is slowed down light

V descending light
W two ways of descending light
X power, empowered
Y awareness
Z as above so below, heaven and earth

WORKING WITH SOUND

Sound is around us all the time and society is created from where the emphasis is placed in sound vibration of our values. Sound can be used for healing and sound too can be a source of stress causing dis-ease. The sound of silence can cleanse our mental clutter. The physical factors which affect us are not nearly as important as the sound vibrations which are coming our way. Abuses are just tests for which we should be thankful and then move on.

The name that we are given at birth is a word which contains the potential possibilities for our life which has just begun. The vowels are the most important part of the name, for they reveal the real power within the word. The consonants give an indication of the direction of and the influence on that power. The first thing, then, which we have to do is to look at the vibration of our names according to the spelling of the name, for here lies our highest potential.

To get into a really close connection with that vibration, first look at the vowels, study their meaning and then, once you have an understanding of their meaning at the mental level, open your airways at a deep level and begin to chant the vowel sounds. The amount of understanding you will glean from this exercise will depend entirely on how much effort you put into it.

To chant, you breathe in through the nose and then chant the sound out through the mouth as you exhale. The longer you chant, the closer you will get to the essence of the vibration and should you decide to fast beforehand, this too will help you to break through any blocks you may have.

Once you have worked on the vowels you will be ready to look at the consonants and these will give you greater understanding of the power of the vowel sounds.

The next aspect of our name to study is the way in which it is pronounced or maybe the sound of the name by which people generally call you. The name sound or word sound that people call us or the sound vibration that is verbalized is what we resonate and therefore is the vibration that we use in turn to bring to us certain situations that will cause us to struggle, because these struggles are the polarities which we call into our lives so that we can reconcile them.

The name 'Jean' contains the vowel sounds 'eh' and 'aaah' but when the word is sounded the predominant vowel sound is 'eeeee' and so Jean would learn that she has a deep connection to placement and purification but that her main issues in life would be in resolving her connection to awareness.

The human psyche is highly suggestible and therefore the advertising media use this factor to their advantage by suggesting that people buy a certain product. They hear the product name over and over again and eventually buy the product.

It is the same with vibrations. If you are being called 'placement' and 'awareness', then your whole life becomes placement and awareness and you call people and situations to yourself which cause you to face placement and awareness.

VOWEL SOUND A, 'AAAAAH', PURIFICATION

When we are in the middle of a task we are not at the beginning or end but out in the middle. Purity enters at that moment to get us unstuck. One of the ways to recognize that purity is working in us is because we were stuck in an issue of fear. One of the best ways to define purity is to see it in action. When we have fear we have purity, they are one and the same thing. One of the qualities of fear is purity and purity creates fear to heal the separation that created the fear that called the beingness of purity to come and heal it. Purity is in the centre, not at the beginning or at the end, purity washes away the separation. Water is a form of purity. The only time we can define purity is when there is separation and it generally appears as the emotion of fear.

VOWEL SOUND E, 'EH', PLACEMENT

When we lose our placement we play by re-creation and then put the four bodies (physical, mental, emotional, spiritual) back into a harmonic balance. Some people seek food, drink, recreation, television, sports or sex, but the main thing here is that the playing connects the person to the heart centre, or their psychological centredness.

Some people take a geographic cure and move to a different area or to a new house or a new job. Some take an emotional cure and move to another relationship but the real issue with placement is that the person is stuck within themselves and until they learn how to make the inward shift then the problems they face in the outside world will be the same problems in different situations. An addiction to alcohol will be replaced by an alternative addiction until the necessity for addiction is overcome. The move must come from within.

VOWEL SOUND I, 'EEE', AWARENESS

When we know we are in awareness the quality of awareness is psychic energy that is moving out and perceiving

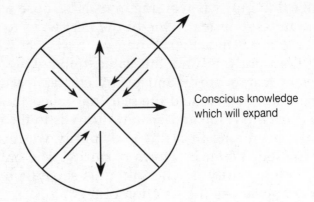

Conscious knowledge
which will expand

what is coming in, so that the characteristic of the ex-
plosive (going out – masculine) rather than implosive
(coming in – feminine) is how one can tell the male and
female cosmic differences.

We have a Divine longing, we thirst for inner truth, we
search for knowledge and wisdom on our path to awareness, hence we have schools, universities, libraries.

VOWEL SOUND O, 'OH', INNOCENCE

Innocence is when you are energy that is going out and
energy that is coming in to the circle of light, and everything in between. When innocence is successfully in your
life you will not hurt those around you, neither will you
be hurt by them. You become like the hollow bone con-
taining only the movement of innocence.

VOWEL SOUND U, 'OOO', CARRYING

We are all carrying things, be they physical, mental, emotional or spiritual. Transport carries us about, women
carry babies into this world and we carry and care for each
other along life's highway.

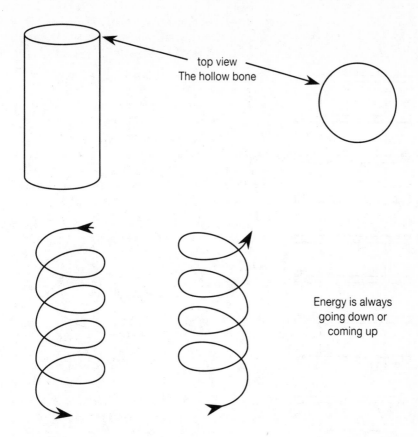

top view
The hollow bone

Energy is always
going down or
coming up

On the medicine wheel, U is at the centre where, having moved through the four directions, we are now ready to be carried to the next level of awareness through transformation of potential.

Each turn on the spiral brings into play different levels of wisdom and what emerges at the top is conscious thought.

The Eternal vastness is all around, constantly changing with stillness. The stepladder leads to insights. Each rung is a heavenly plane connection. We are creating our pasts as we are changing our futures.

The process by which insight enters into the hollow

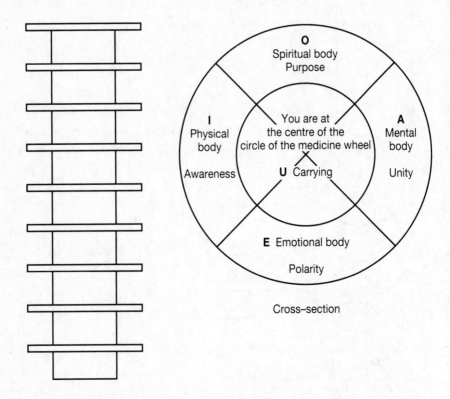

Cross–section

tube, which is made of mental, emotional, physical and spiritual bodies, is by the rungs on the stepladder and we use the consonant L because it connects us to the heavenly plane. The heavenly plane contains the future and also essences of the ancient past, hence parallel universes of awareness.

3   Discovering Your Essence Name

IN THE MYTHIC VIEW OF creation, in the beginning the Creator fills the infinite space of the vast self with his laughter of joyous beauty. And in that making of beauty it is said that the laughter resonated out to all four corners of the vast infinite self that created the mental, emotional, physical and spiritual laws that were to govern the unfolding of the vastness of the Divine self. In the context of this ever-unfolding beauty, the Creator, having finished this step in creation, transforms himself into the Tao of the constant Isness and the constant becomingness of life and then chooses to come forth to join the People's vibration on his/their journey back home.

At this point, the storytellers tell us, some of the people went to the East and some went to the South and some went to the North.

However, the People who went to the West became the people of the physical worlds, to live there until such time as they might return to the centre of the circle-of-light of their origin. The voices of the People's Divine longing to return home created the physical beingness of Waa-Maa-Chi. The breath materialized Divine Longingness of the heart and Divine Longingness became the basis for the being to return to the Divine Origin to which everything in time returns.

The physical oceans on the earth can be said to represent the lungs of the planet which cleanse and purify the breath of the planet's materialization of matter through the motion of movement. As the earth moves and rotates around the physical sun it calls forth the solar winds that bring forth our four seasons of Winter, Spring, Summer and Autumn. Similarly we are born into the time of our season and having matured into beyond the Autumn time, we cross through an opening crack between two slices of light into our Winter season of 'The ever-unfolding motion of the dreaming heart of the ever-loving beingness'.

When a physical person is born they come to bring Breath (Winter), Materialism and Movement (Spring, Summer and Autumn) into reality because the breath is the entity that gives the person their name and hence, through the letters, the connection to the inspiration of insights. The breath connects the individual to the spirit of inspiration; that aspect of the inner life of the breath that produces the insights that appear on the surface but are rooted in the inner depths of the innermost self. This is the essence of the metaphorical mind.

Then the breath carries life to materialism; one could say it is the physical manifestation of the creative unfolding or expression of that which has been inspired through the breath and is the physical experience of the person whose name is unfolding cosmically. Movement creates the ever-changing perceptions in the context of life as the person is moving toward greater and greater levels of higher self learning.

In summary, the breath is the name giver and identifies the letters in the name that are to be given to the new person and then gives the person their name in letters, the letters (the consonants and vowels) by which they are to be known. The person's goals and objectives will materialize alongside these experiences brought into flow or conflict in order to create the dynamics or shifts for change to occur. And movement is created in the process in order to see how the metaphoric alongside the experiences can be understood as revelations of the person's unfolding.

Practice

At this point in the book we want to recommend that you find your personal inner source of inspiration by finding and singing your song, making a dance for it and then using them both by applying them to your ceremonial rituals for the greater enhancement of your personal self growth.

First of all, start by making a note of the vowels in your name and study how the essences of the vowels may be influencing your life. Secondly, chant the vowel sounds out loud. Then notice the images, thoughts and visions that come to you once you start chanting – these will determine the dance that you will perform.

Next, pay attention to the sound of the song of your name because soon within the sound there will appear an intuition or an actual image of a being that will begin to demonstrate your personal dance.

Take time to create the necessary physical steps for your dance ritual and once you have created it and sung to it as you are dancing it, ask it to help you to become a better human.

The quiet pool

Use your song and dance by putting them into the cadence of the 1–2, 1–2 of a silence that begins to descend into the inner senses of your mind and while watching it, see where it stops as it drops into a pool of 'quiet waters made of new beginnings'. This pool will give you intuitive meanings of your next direction or introduce you to a new start in your life.

Studying the breath is important because in the inhalation the chanter owns everything he has been and has become up until that point in his life, and in the exhalation the chanter releases them.

The breathing must be continued until such time as the images and the intuitions begin to emerge quite clearly.

The column of light

In another practice, imagine yourself moving up inside a column of white light. Keep your attention on rising up until the raising force stops of its own volition, at which time two two-legged beings will appear and will address you and your needs and will give advice regarding your current state of affairs.

The medicine wheel

Another technique is to imagine sitting in the centre of the medicine wheel. Start by facing the direction of the East and singing your medicine song silently in order to call in the infinite awareness of the medicine wheel which will begin to respond to your beingness because your beingness is known to the breath of inspiration. Consequently it will send mental healing or mental formulations from the East and it will send emotional healing or feeling type impulses from the South. The West will be inspired to heal your physicalities and the North will send healing towards your spiritual body.

See the medicine wheel on page 9 for a better intellectual understanding of how to use the A-E-I-O-U letters within the circle.

4   Practical Applications

TWO PRACTICAL ACTIONS NECESSARY for reaching the results that you can expect through your journey of self-discovery are the give-away and fasting because the give-away will remove any mental, emotional or spiritual blocks and fasting will open you to receiving insights of knowing from your inner self.

First take a personal inventory of people you may have harmed and mentally ask for their forgiveness, if you cannot do it in person. Secondly take some quiet time to search for any mental, emotional or spiritual blocks that may be keeping you in bondage as well. Thirdly seek for some physical personal item, such as jewellery, that you are really fond of and which you cherish and would like to keep. Take the article and give it away to a total stranger with love.

This type of action will clear all mental, emotional or spiritual blocks because the energies of your mental, emotional, physical and spiritual bodies will be released and your physical body will be free-flowing again, as you will almost immediately see and feel in its movement.

Fasting for at least eight hours before seeking to find your song and your dance is important because while fasting your physical body will be in a greater state of receptivity and will be open to incoming realizations from the inner wisdom regarding your quest for your personal truth.

Finally, develop the gift of giving as a personal routine in your life so that you give about four times a year. Discipline yourself so that you continue to fast at least once a week in order to develop a strong connection to the spiritual source of personal inspiration.

In summary, remove all personal blockages through the gift of giving and fast regularly in order to keep yourself as an open channel of receptivity.

HOW INSPIRATION APPEARS

After chanting your personal sound, practise listening to the silence, the sound of the silence of the sound you have just chanted, and wait for inspiration to appear out of the silence. And in metaphor, silence is that place where all knowing arises from and nurtures the essence of beingness.

The true seeker will act on what is given and in that act alone the commitment of the initiate will bring forth the strength and vitality to further explore the inner knowing that is overflowing with wisdom of esoteric thought.

This is one method of reaching the stillness of the small voice that speaks out of the inner recesses of the intuition, the life source of the inspiration. The goal of breath which manifests as the metaphoric mind is to bring forth personal living experiences to you so that you may achieve your own highest potential.

Allow the inspirations in your life to care for your highest potential at any given moment, so that you may live wisely.

DANCING STEPS

Only one type of dance movement is suggested here as we leave for you the delight of finding and then applying your own dance movements.

The forward and backward movement is the metaphoric meaning of worship, the Divine essence of your life. Be sure to put worship at the very top of your list because as you grow in the worship of your inner life so will your devotion grow for the all the experiences in your life. And in time you will see yourself as a devotee to all the moments of your living activities of your daily experiences. Soon thereafter you will become more and more aware that surrounding your normal life is an undying grace made of a noble and deep beauty which will be there guiding and caring for you in an intimate personalized way. It will be the Divine presence of the Beautiful One always yielding and always giving to you personally.

Now you know how to use the book and how to apply the metaphor to the words, you can start looking at the names of your friends, foods, flowers, trees, etc.

In Appendix 1 you will find a list of everyday words with their dictionary definition alongside their metaphor meaning. This should help you to apply the understanding that you have learnt in this book. Appendix 2 lists some common gemstones and gives their corresponding metaphors.

5 A to Z of Common Names and Their Meanings

(*Note*: Italic denotes historical meanings)

Aaron   is the purity that purifies the radiating light of childlike innocence of the self. *Possibly Hebrew '(a) light'.*

Abigail   is purification of path of awareness and goodness of the purity of awareness of the ascending light. *Hebrew 'father's joy'.*

Abraham   is purity of sacred path of the radiating light which purifies as it rises up God's stepladder to beyond the beyond and purifies all that is manifest. *Father of a multitude.*

Ada   is the purity of creation purified. *Origin obscure.*

Adair   is the purity that purifies creation and washes all that is manifest. *Scottish version of Edgar.*

Adam   is the purity that purifies creation and purifies all that is brought forth. *Hebrew 'man'.*

Adamina   is the purity that purifies creation and purifies all that is brought forth bringing awareness to the infinite self purified. *Fem. form of Adam.*

Adele   is purification of creation echoing the ascending light and reflecting it. *Germanic 'noble'*.

Adrian   is the purification of creation radiating awareness through purity of the self. *Latin 'of the Adriatic'*.

Africa   is purity of faith radiating the light of awareness of beauty which is purified. *Celtic 'pleasant'*.

Agatha   is the purification of goodness and purification of time rising up God's stepladder to beyond the beyond in purity. *Greek 'good'*.

Agnes   is purity and goodness of the self echoing one half of eternity. *Greek 'pure'*.

Aileen   is purity and awareness of ascending light reflected which is then reflected by the infinite self. *Irish form of Helen*.

Ailsa   is purifying awareness of the ascending light of one half of eternity purified. *Scottish version of Elsa*.

Alan   is purification of the ascending light which purifies the infinite self. *Ancient Celtic*.

Albert   is purification of the ascending light, following the sacred path of reflecting light and radiating crystallized light. *Germanic 'noble and bright'*.

Alexander is purifying the ascending light, echoing power and purifying the self and then creating reflections of radiating light. *Greek 'defender of men'*.

Alexandra is purifying the ascending light, echoing power and purifying the self and creating the radiating light of purity. *Fem. form of Alexander*.

Alexis   is purification of ascending light reflecting the power of awareness of one half of eternity. *Greek 'helper'*.

Alfred   is the purity of the ascending light of faith radiating the light of reflection of creation. *Old English 'elf counsel' or 'old peace'.*

Alice   is the purity of ascending light with awareness of the beauty of reflections. *Germanic 'nobility'.*

Alison   is the purifying of ascending light in awareness of one half of eternity and through childlike innocence of the self. *Version of Alice.*

Alistair   is purifying the ascending light in awareness of one half of eternity and through time purifying awareness of the radiating light. *Version of Alexander.*

Alma   is purification of ascending light bringing faith to purity. *Russian place name.*

Althea   is purification of ascending light of time, rising up God's stepladder reflecting purity. *Greek 'healthy'.*

Amanda   is the purity which brings forth purity of the self and creates the light of purity. *Latin 'fit to be loved'.*

Amelia   is purity which brings forth reflections of the ascending light in awareness of purity. *Form of Emily.*

Amy   is purity of bringing forth awareness. *Latin 'a woman beloved'.*

Andrea   is the purified self creating radiating light which then reflects purity. *Fem. form of Andrew.*

Andrew   is the pure self creating radiating light which reflects the essence of descending light. *Greek 'manly'.*

Angela   is the purified self and goodness of reflections of the ascending light purified. *Greek 'angel'.*

Angus   is the purified self with the goodness that

carries one half of eternity. *Gaelic 'unique choice'*.

Ann   is purification of the finite and infinite self. *Hebrew 'grace'*.

Anthea   is purity of the self and crystallized light rising up God's stepladder and reflecting purity. *Greek 'a flower'*.

Anthony   is the pure self allowing crystallized light to rise up God's stepladder to the heavenly planes in childlike innocence of the self and its own awareness. *Latin 'strength'*.

April   is purity of the heart which radiates awareness of the ascending light. *Month name.*

Archibald   is purity of radiance of beauty rising up God's stepladder to the heavenly planes with awareness of path of beauty of the ascending light of creativity. *Germanic 'true and bold'*.

Arlene   is purity of the radiance of the ascending light mirroring the self in reflection. *Possibly Celtic 'pledge'*.

Arnold   is purity of the radiating light of the self and childlike innocence of the ascending light of creation. *Germanic 'eagle and ruler'*.

Arthur   is purification of the radiating light and through time rising up God's stepladder to the heavenly planes, carrying the light which radiates. *Celtic, meaning obscure.*

Asa   is the purity of one half of eternity purified. *Hebrew 'God heals'*.

Audrey   is the purity which carries creativity, radiating echoes of awareness. *Old English 'noble and mighty'*.

Avril   is the purity of the descending light radiating awareness of the ascending light. *Version of April.*

Barbara   is the pathway to purity of the radiating light and the heavenly path to complete purity of the radiating light. *Greek 'foreign'*.

Barnaby   is the path to purity of the radiating light which through the self purifies the path of awareness. *Hebrew 'son of exhortation'*.

Barry   is the heavenly path to purity of the radiating light which radiates awareness. *Irish 'spearman'*.

Beatrice   is the path of the reflective universe purifying time and radiating awareness of beauty in reflectivity. *Latin 'bringer of joy'*.

Belinda   is the path of reflection of the ascending light in awareness of the self creating purity. *Italian and Germanic 'beautiful serpent'*.

Benjamin   is the path of reflection of the self, seeing purity and bringing forth awareness of the self. *Hebrew 'son of the right hand'*.

Bernard   is the path of reflection of the radiating light of the self purifying the radiance of creation. *Germanic 'warrior' or 'bear, strong'*.

Bernadette   is the path of reflection of the reflection of the radiating light of the self purifying creation and mirroring the crystallized light in time of reflection. *Fem. form of Bernard*.

Bernice   is the path of reflection of the radiating light of the self and awareness of the beauty of reflection. *Greek 'victory bringer'*.

Beryl   is the path of reflection of the radiating light in awareness of the ascending light. *Jewel name*.

Betty   is the path of reflection of time and time of awareness. *Version of Elizabeth*.

Bill   is the path of awareness of two ways of ascending light. *Version of William*.

Brenda   is the sacred path of radiating light reflecting the self and creating purity. *Scandinavian, fem. form of Brand, 'sword'.*

Brian is the sacred path of the radiating light of awareness purifying the self. *Celtic 'strong'.*

Bridget is the sacred path of the radiating light of awareness creating goodness in the echoes of time. *Irish 'lofty' or 'august'.*

Bronwen is the sacred path of radiating light in childlike innocence of the self and descending light twice over reflecting the self. *Welsh 'whitebreasted'.*

Bruce is the sacred path radiating and carrying beauty reflected. *Norman place name.*

Calum is the beauty that purifies the ascending light and carries matter. *Pet form of Malcolm.*

Camilla is the beauty which is purified and bringing forth of awareness of the two ways of ascending light which is purified. *Latin 'noble maiden fit to serve in temple'.*

Cara is the beauty of purity radiating the light of purity. *Irish 'friend'.*

Carl is the beauty of the purity of the radiating and ascending light. *Version of Charles.*

Carol is the beauty which purifies the radiating light in childlike innocence of the ascending light. *Fem. form of Charles.*

Caroline is the beauty which purifies the radiating light in childlike innocence of the ascending light in awareness of the self in reflection. *Fem. form of Charles.*

Cassandra is beauty which purifies one half of eternity and in the other half of eternity purifies the self creating and radiating the light of purity. *Greek 'helper of men'.*

Catherine is beauty purifying time up God's stepladder, reflecting the radiating light in awareness of the self reflective. *Greek 'pure'*.

Catriona   is beauty purifying time, radiating awareness of the childlike innocence of the self purified. *Gaelic Catherine*.

Cecil   is beauty reflecting the beauty of awareness of the ascending light. *Latin 'blind'*.

Celia   is the beauty which reflects the ascending light in awareness of purity. *Fem. form of Cecil*.

Charity   is the beauty which rises up God's stepladder purifying the radiating light in awareness of the time of awareness. *Christian 'virtue'*.

Charles   is the beauty of rising up God's stepladder washing the radiating light in the ascending light of awareness of one half of eternity. *Old High German 'freeman'*.

Charlotte   is beauty which rises up God's stepladder and purifies the radiating light in the ascending light of childlike innocence in two ways of time reflected. *Fem. form of Charles*.

Christine   is beauty rising up God's stepladder radiating the light of awareness of one half of eternity in time of awareness of the self in reflection. *From Latin 'Christus'*.

Christopher   is beauty rising up God's stepladder radiating awareness of one half of eternity and in the time of childlike innocence of the heart, rising up God's stepladder to reflect the radiating light. *Greek 'he who bore Christ'*.

Claire   is the beauty of the ascending light purifying awareness and radiating reflection. *Latin 'renowned'*.

Cleopatra   is the beauty of the ascending light reflecting the childlike innocence of the heart, purifying time and radiating the light of purity. *Greek 'glory of one's father'*.

Clifford   is the beauty of the ascending light in

awareness of faith and faith in childlike innocence radiating the light of creativity. *Surname, place name.*

Clive   is beauty of the ascending light in awareness of the descending light reflected. *Old English 'cliff, slope, river bank'.*

Colin   is the beauty of childlike innocence of the ascending light in awareness of the self. *Latin 'dove'.*

Connor   is the beauty of the childlike innocence of the planetary and infinite self and childlike innocence of the radiating light. *Irish 'high will, courage'.*

Conrad   is the beauty of childlike innocence of the self radiating the light of the beauty of creation. *Germanic 'bold and counsel'.*

Cora   is the beauty of childlike innocence radiating the light of purity. *Irish 'a maiden'.*

Craig   is beauty radiating purity of awareness of goodness. *Scottish surname, 'crag, cliff'.*

Cuthbert   is beauty which carries time up God's stepladder and along the path of reflection of the radiance of crystallized light. *Old English 'famous and bright'.*

Cynthia   is beauty of awareness of the self in time rising up God's stepladder to awareness of purity. *Latin 'the goddess'.*

Cyril   is beauty of awareness radiating awareness of the ascending light. *Greek 'lordly'.*

Daisy   is creating purity of awareness of one half of eternity in awareness. *Flower name, Old English 'day's eye'.*

Daniel   is the creation of purity of the self and awareness of the reflections of the ascending light. *Hebrew 'God is my judge'.*

Daphne   is the creation of purification of the heart, and rising up God's stepladder to the self reflected. *Greek 'bay tree'.*

Darren   is the creation of purity of the radiating light which radiates reflections on the self. *Surname.*

Daryl   is the creation of purity of the radiating light and awareness of the ascending light. *Middle English place name.*

David   is creation of the purity of the descending light and awareness of creation. *Hebrew 'beloved'.*

Dawn   is the creation of purity of two ways of descending light of the self. *From the dawn.*

Deborah   is the creation of reflection along the path of childlike innocence, radiating purification which rises up God's stepladder to the heavenly planes. *Hebrew 'a bee'.*

Deidre   is creation mirroring awareness and radiating the light of creation and radiating reflection. *Celtic 'the raging one'.*

Delia   is the creation of reflections of the ascending light in awareness of purity. *Greek, originally surname of the goddess Artemis.*

Denise   is the creation of mirrors of the self and awareness of one half of eternity in reflection. *Fem. form of Dennis.*

Dennis   is the creation of reflections of the self and awareness of one half of eternity. *From Dionysus, the Greek god.*

Derek   is the creation of mirrors of radiating light reflecting God's planting fields. *Germanic 'people and ruler'.*

Desmond   is the creation of reflections of one half of eternity and the bringing forth of childlike innocence of the self in creativity. *Irish clan name.*

Diana   is creating awareness of purification of the self purified. *Roman goddess of the moon*.

Diane   is creating awareness of purity of self reflected. *Version of Diana*.

Dick   is creating awareness of beauty and planting it in God's planting fields. *Pet form of Richard*.

Digby   is the creation of awareness of goodness along the sacred path to awareness. *Surname*.

Donald   creates childlike innocence of the self and purifies the ascending light of creation. *Gaelic 'world ruler'*.

Donna   creates childlike innocence of the finite and infinite self purified. *Italian 'lady, mistress'*.

Doris   creates childlike innocence and radiates the light of awareness through one half of eternity. *Greek 'a girl'*.

Dorothy   is creating childlike innocence, radiating innocence and in time rising up God's stepladder to awareness. *Greek 'gift of God'*.

Dougal   creates childlike innocence and carries the goodness which purifies the ascending light. *Celtic 'swarthy stranger'*.

Douglas   is creating childlike innocence, carrying goodness through the ascending light which purifies one half of eternity. *Celtic 'dark blue'*.

Dudley   is creation which carries the creation of the ascending light which reflects awareness. *Surname*.

Duncan   is creativity carrying the self and beauty purifying self. *Celtic 'brown warrior'*.

Dylan   is creating awareness of the ascending light in the purity of the self. *Welsh 'sea'*.

Eamon   is reflections of purity bringing forth childlike innocence of the self. *Irish form of Edmund*.

Edgar	is echoes of the creation of goodness purifying the radiating light. *Old English 'prosperity and spear'*.
Edith	is reflecting creation of awareness through time up God's stepladder. *Old English 'prosperity and warlike'*.
Edmund	is reflections of creation bringing forth and carrying the self in creativity. *Old English 'prosperity and protection'*.
Edna	is reflecting creation of the self purified. *Fem. form of Edwin*.
Edward	is reflecting the creation of two ways of descending light purifying the radiance of creation. *Old English 'treasure and guardian'*.
Edwin	is reflecting the creation of two ways of descending light in awareness of the self. *Old English 'prosperity and friend'*.
Eileen	is reflections of awareness of the ascending light reflecting twice over in the self. *Celtic form of Helen*.
Elaine	is reflections of the ascending light purifying awareness of the self in reflectivity. *Version of Helen*.
Eleanor	is reflections of the ascending light mirroring purity of the self and innocently radiating light. *Version of Helen*.
Elizabeth	is the reflection of the ascending light of awareness of the heavenly and earthly planes, purifying the path to reflection of the time of rising up God's stepladder to beyond the beyond. *Hebrew 'consecrated to God'*.
Ellen	reflects two ways of ascending light and mirrors the self. *Version of Helen*.
Elma	is reflections of ascending light bringing forth purity. *Fem. form of Spanish saint*.
Elsa	is reflections of ascending light of one half of eternity purified. *Pet form of Elizabeth*.

Elspeth   is reflections of ascending light of one half of eternity and from the heart reflecting time and rising up God's stepladder. *Scottish form of Elizabeth.*

Emily   is the reflecting light which brings forth awareness in the ascending light of awareness. *Roman clan name.*

Emma   is the reflection of bringing purity forth twice over. *Shortened German name 'all embracing'.*

Ena   is reflecting the self in purity. *Form of Edna.*

Enid   is reflections of self and awareness of creation. *Celtic 'spotless purity'.*

Eric   is reflecting the radiating light of awareness of beauty. *Scandinavian 'ever ruler'.*

Ernest   is mirroring the radiating light of the self and reflecting one half of eternity through time. *From 'earnestness'.*

Esmerelda   is reflection of one half of eternity bringing forth reflections of radiating light, reflecting the ascending light and creating purity. *Spanish 'emerald'.*

Esther   is reflecting one half of eternity through time and rising up God's stepladder to reflect the radiating light. *Hebrew 'myrtle'.*

Ethel   is reflecting time up God's stepladder and mirroring the ascending light. *Old English 'noble'.*

Eunice   is reflecting and carrying the self in awareness of beauty which is mirrored. *Greek 'good victory'.*

Eva   is reflecting the descending light in purity. *Hebrew 'life giving'.*

Evelyn   is reflecting the descending light and reflecting the ascending light in awareness of the self. *From Celtic 'pleasant'.*

Ewan   is reflecting two ways of descending light purifying the self. *From Celtic 'young warrior'.*

Fabian
is faith in purity on the sacred path of awareness and purity of the self. *Roman clan name.*

Faith
is faith in the purity of awareness through time rising up God's stepladder to beyond. *Christian virtue.*

Fay
is faith in the purity of awareness. *Form of Faith.*

Felicity
is faith in the reflection of ascending light of awareness and the beauty of awareness in the time of awareness. *From Latin 'happiness.*

Fergus
is faith in reflections of the radiating light and the goodness of carrying one half of eternity. *Celtic 'man and choice'.*

Finbar
is faith in awareness of the self and sacred path to purity of the radiating light. *Irish.*

Fiona
is faith in the awareness of childlike innocence of the self purified. *From Gaelic 'white'.*

Flora
is faith in the ascending light and the child-like innocence of the radiating light purified. *Roman goddess of flowers and Spring.*

Frances
is faith in the radiating light which purifies the self and the beauty of reflection of one half of eternity. *From Germanic 'free'.*

Francesca
is faith in the radiating light of purity of the self and of the beauty of the echoes of one half of eternity and the beauty of purity. *From Frances.*

Frank
is faith radiating the light of purity of the self and planting it. *From Francis, masc. form of Frances.*

Freda
is faith radiating the light of reflections of creation and purifying it. *Pet form of Winifred.*

Frederick
is faith radiating the light of reflections of creation. *Germanic 'peace and ruler'.*

Freya   is faith in the radiating light reflecting awareness of purity. *Norse goddess of love.*

Gail   is the goodness of purity and awareness of the ascending light. *From Abigail.*

Gareth   is goodness of purity radiating reflections through time up God's stepladder. *Germanic 'ravages'.*

Gary   is goodness of purity radiating the light of awareness. *Pet form of Gareth.*

Gay   is the goddess of purity of awareness. *From the adjective.*

Geoffrey   is the goodness which is reflected in childlike innocence of faith twice over, and radiating the reflections of awareness. *Germanic 'God and peace'.*

George   is goodness reflecting childlike innocence and radiating the goodness of reflection. *Greek 'earth worker'.*

Gerald   is goodness which reflects the radiating light, purifying the ascending light of creation. *Germanic 'spear wielder'.*

Gerard   is goodness which reflects the radiating light purifying the radiating of creation. *Germanic 'spear and hard'.*

Gertrude   is goodness reflecting radiating and time radiating the light of carrying creation in reflection. *Germanic 'spear and beloved'.*

Gideon   is the goodness of awareness creating reflections of childlike innocence of the self. *Hebrew 'destroyer'.*

Gilbert   is the goodness of awareness of the ascending light along the path which reflects the radiating light of time. *Germanic 'hostage and bright'.*

Giles   is the goodness of awareness of the ascending light which reflects one half of eternity. *Greek 'a kid'.*

Gillian   is goodness of awareness of two ways of ascending light and awareness of purity of the self. *From Juliana.*

Gladys   is goodness of the ascending light of purity of creation and awareness of one half of eternity. *Welsh form of Claudia.*

Godfrey   is the goodness of the childlike innocence of creation with faith in the radiating light which reflects awareness. *Same as Geoffrey.*

Gordon   is the goodness of childlike innocence which radiates the light creativity in childlike innocence of the self. *Scottish surname.*

Grace   is the goodness of the radiating light of purity in the beauty of reflection. *From 'divine grace'.*

Graham   is goodness radiating purity up God's stepladder and the purifying of manifestation. *Celtic surname.*

Gregor   is the goodness radiating reflection and goodness of the childlike innocence of the radiating light. *Greek 'watchman'.*

Greta   is goodness radiating reflections of time purified. *Pet form of Margaret.*

Guy   is goodness carrying awareness. *Germanic 'wood'.*

Gwenda   is goodness of two ways of descending light reflecting the self and creating purity. *Celtic 'white'.*

Hamish   is rising up God's stepladder in purity, bringing forth awareness of one half of eternity and taking it up God's stepladder to beyond the beyond. *Gaelic form of James.*

Hank   is rising up God's stepladder in purity of the self and planting it in God's planting fields. *American pet form of Henry.*

Harry   is rising up God's stepladder in the purity of the radiating light and radiating awareness. *Form of Harold or Henry.*

Hazel   is rising up God's stepladder in the purity of the heavenly and earthly planes and reflecting the ascending light. *From the tree.*

Heather   is rising up God's stepladder echoing the purity of time and rising up again to reflect the radiating light. *From the shrub.*

Helen   is rising up God's stepladder reflecting the ascending light and then mirroring the self. *Greek 'bright'.*

Henry   is rising up God's stepladder to beyond the beyond reflecting the self and radiating awareness. *Old High German 'home and ruler'.*

Herbert   is rising up God's stepladder, reflecting the radiating light and taking the sacred path to reflect that radiance through time. *Old English 'army and bright'.*

Hester   is rising up God's stepladder reflecting one half of eternity and through time reflecting the radiating light. *Version of Esther.*

Hilary   is rising up God's stepladder to awareness of the ascending light, purifying the radiating light in awareness. *Latin 'cheerful'.*

Hilda   is rising up God's stepladder to awareness of the ascending light and creating purity. *Germanic 'battle'.*

Hope   is rising up God's stepladder in childlike innocence and then reflecting it from the heart. *Christian virtue.*

Horace   is rising up God's stepladder in childlike innocence radiating the light of purity into beauty which is mirrored. *Roman name.*

Hugh
is rising up God's stepladder and carrying goodness up the ladder to beyond the beyond. *Germanic 'mind, thought'.*

Humphrey
is rising up God's stepladder carrying all that is manifest in the heart and rising up God's stepladder radiating reflections of awareness. *Germanic 'giant and peace'.*

Ian
is awareness of the purity of the self. *Gaelic form of John.*

Ilona
is awareness of the ascending light of the childlike innocence of the self purified. *Scottish name.*

Ina
is awareness of the self purified. *Pet name.*

Inga
is awareness of the self and goodness which is purified. *Scandinavian name.*

Ingrid
is awareness of the self and goodness radiating the light of awareness of creation. *Norwegian 'fair one'.*

Innes
is awareness of the self and the self reflecting one half of eternity. *Gaelic 'island'.*

Iona
is awareness of the childlike innocence of the self purified. *Scottish island.*

Irene
is awareness of the radiating light mirrored and the self reflected. *Greek 'peace'.*

Iris
is awareness of the radiating light and awareness of one half of eternity. *Greek 'rainbow'.*

Isabel
is the awareness of one half of eternity purifying the sacred path reflecting the ascending light. *Version of Elizabeth.*

Isla
is the awareness of one half of eternity and ascending light purified. *Scottish 'river'.*

Ivan
is the awareness of the descending light which purifies the self. *Russian form of John.*

Jacob is the eyes that see purity of beauty in childlike innocence. *Hebrew 'a supplanter'.*

Jacqueline is seeing the purity of beauty and initiating the carrying of reflections of the ascending light in awareness of the self reflected. *Fem. form of French Jacques.*

James is seeing the purity of bringing forth reflections of one half of eternity. *Hebrew origin, uncertain meaning.*

Jane is seeing the purity of the self reflected. *Fem. form of John.*

Janet is seeing the purity of the self reflected in crystallized light. *Form of Jane.*

Janice is seeing purity of the self in awareness of beauty which is reflected. *Form of Jane.*

Jasmine is seeing the purity of one half of eternity and bringing forth awareness of the self reflected. *Flower name.*

Jason is seeing the purity of one half of eternity in childlike innocence of the self. *Hebrew 'the Lord is my salvation'.*

Jean is seeing reflections of the beauty of the self. *Form of Jane.*

Jeffery is seeing the reflections of faith and faith in the radiating light echoed in awareness. *Version of Geoffrey.*

Jemima is seeing reflections of bringing forth awareness and bringing forth purity. *Hebrew 'dove'.*

Jennifer is seeing reflections of self and the self being aware of faith, in the reflection of the radiating light. *Cornish name.*

Jeremy is seeing reflections of the radiating light and reflecting the bringing forth of awareness. *Hebrew 'Jehovah has appointed'.*

Jessica is seeing reflections of two halves of eternity on awareness of beauty which is purified. *Hebrew 'God is looking'.*

Joan is seeing in childlike innocence and purifying the self. *From Johanna, Hebrew 'God is gracious'.*

John is seeing in childlike innocence and rising up God's stepladder to the self. *Hebrew 'God is gracious'.*

Jonathan is seeing in childlike innocence of the self, purifying time and rising up God's stepladder to purification of the self. *Hebrew 'Jehovah's gift'.*

Joseph is seeing in childlike innocence one half of eternity and reflecting it through the heart and up God's stepladder to beyond the beyond. *Hebrew 'he shall add'.*

Josephine is seeing in childlike innocence one half of eternity and reflecting it through the heart and up God's stepladder to beyond the beyond in awareness of the self reflected. *Fem. form of Joseph.*

Joy is seeing with eyes of childlike innocence and awareness. *A virtue.*

Joyce is seeing with the eyes of childlike innocence and awareness the beauty of reflections. *A Breton saint.*

Judith is the eyes that see the carrying of creativity in awareness of time up God's stepladder to beyond the beyond. *Hebrew 'a Jewess'.*

Julia is the eyes that carry the ascending light in awareness of purity. *Latin, fem. form of Julius.*

Julie is the eyes that carry the ascending light in awareness of reflection. *Form of Julia.*

June is seeing the carrying of self reflected. *Month name.*

Karen is planting purity and radiating reflections of the self. *Danish form of Catherine.*

Kate   is planting the purity of time reflected. *Pet form of Catherine.*

Kay   is planting purity of awareness. *Welsh name, Arthurian knight.*

Keith   is planting reflections of awareness of time and rising up God's stepladder to beyond the beyond. *Surname, place name.*

Kenneth   is planting reflections of the self and through the self reflecting time up God's stepladder. *Celtic 'fair one'.*

Kerry   is planting reflections of the radiating light and radiating the light of awareness. *Irish place name.*

Kevin   is planting reflections of the descending light in awareness of the self. *Old Irish 'dear birth'.*

Kim   is planting the awareness of manifestation. *From Kimberley, place name.*

Kirsty   is planting awareness of the radiance of one half of eternity in time of awareness. *Scottish form of Christine.*

Lachlan   is the ascending light purifying beauty and rising up God's stepladder and the ascending light purifying the self. *Gaelic name.*

Laura   is the ascending light of purity carrying the radiating light which is purified. *Fem. form of Laurence, 'laurel'.*

Lee   is the ascending light reflected twice over. *Place name.*

Leila   is the ascending light reflecting awareness and the ascending light purified. *Persian name.*

Leonard   is the ascending light reflecting the childlike innocence of the self purifying the radiance of creation. *Germanic 'lion and hard'.*

Lesley	is the ascending light reflecting one half of eternity and the ascending light reflecting awareness. *Surname.*
Lewis	is the ascending light reflecting two ways of descending light in awareness of one half of eternity. *From French Louis; also Scottish island.*
Liam	is the ascending light of awareness purifying manifestation. *Irish form of William.*
Lilith	is the ascending light of awareness twice over and a time to rise up God's stepladder to the heavenly planes. *Hebrew 'vampire'.*
Lillian	is the ascending light of awareness twice over, purifying the self. *Latin 'lily'.*
Lily	is the ascending light of awareness twice over. *Flower name.*
Linda	is the ascending light of awareness of the self creating purity. *Spanish 'beautiful, pretty'.*
Lindsay	is the ascending light of awareness of the self creating for half of eternity purity of awareness. *Scottish clan and place name.*
Lionel	is the ascending light of awareness of the childlike innocence of the self reflected in the ascending light. *Latin 'lion'.*
Lisa	is the ascending light of awareness of one half of eternity purified. *Pet form of Elizabeth.*
Lorna	is the ascending light of childlike innocence radiating the light of the self purified. *First mentioned in the book 'Lorna Doone'.*
Lorraine	is the ascending light of childlike innocence radiating twice over purity and awareness of the self purified. *French place name.*
Louise	is the ascending light of childlike innocence carrying awareness of one half of eternity and reflecting it. *Fem. form of French Louis.*
Lucy	is the ascending light carrying beauty of awareness. *Latin 'light'.*

Lydia is the ascending light of awareness creating awareness purified. *Greek '(a woman) of Lydia'.*

Lynne is the ascending light of awareness of the self twice over and the reflections of it. *Celtic 'a pool'.*

Mabel is bringing forth purity of the sacred path and reflecting the ascending light. *English form of Amabel.*

Madeleine is bringing forth purity, creating reflections of the radiating light in awareness of the self reflected. *Hebrew '(a woman) of Magdala'.*

Mairi is bringing forth purity of awareness and radiating awareness. *Gaelic form of Mary.*

Malcolm is bringing forth purity in the ascending light and the beauty of childlike innocence of the ascending light which is manifest. *Gaelic 'a disciple of Colum'.*

Marcia is bringing forth purity of radiance in the beauty of awareness of purification. *Fem. form of Marcus, 'Mars'.*

Margaret is bringing forth purity of the radiating light and the goodness of purity of the radiating light which reflects time. *Greek 'a pearl'.*

Maria is bringing forth purity of the radiating light with awareness which is purified. *Version of Mary.*

Marie is bringing forth purity of the radiating light with awareness which is reflected. *Version of Mary.*

Marilyn is bringing forth purity of the radiating light with awareness and the ascending light of awareness of the self. *Version of Mary.*

Marion   is bringing forth purity of the radiating light of awareness in childlike innocence of the self. *Version of Mary.*

Marissa   is bringing forth purity of the radiating light in awareness of one half of eternity which is purified. *Version of Mary.*

Marjory   is bringing forth purity of the radiating light and seeing in childlike innocence the radiating light of awareness. *Version of Margaret.*

Mark   is bringing forth purity of radiance and planting it. *Latin, one of the four Gospel writers.*

Marlene   is bringing forth purification of the radiating light and reflecting the ascending light and reflecting the self. *Version of Magdalena.*

Martha   is bringing forth purity of the radiating light and through time rising up God's stepladder in purity. *Aramaic 'lady'.*

Martin   is bringing forth purity of the radiating light and through time finding awareness of the self. *Mars, Roman god of war.*

Mary   is bringing forth purity, radiance and awareness. *Greek form of Miriam, 'wished for child'.*

Matilda   is bringing forth purity and, through time, awareness of the ascending light of creation purified. *Germanic 'might and battle'.*

Matthew   is bringing forth purity of crystallized light and through time rising up God's stepladder reflecting two ways of descending light. *Hebrew 'gift of Jehovah'.*

Maureen   is bringing forth purity, carrying the radiating light reflected and reflecting the self. *Irish form of Mary.*

Maurice   is bringing forth the purity of carrying the radiating light in awareness of beauty reflected. *Latin 'a moor'.*

May	is bringing forth purity of awareness. *Month name*.
Melanie	is bringing forth reflections of the ascending light purifying the self in awareness of reflection. *Greek 'black'*.
Merlin	brings forth reflections of radiating and ascending light bringing awareness to the self. *Welsh legendary name*.
Michael	is bringing forth awareness of beauty rising up God's stepladder purifying reflections of the ascending light. *Hebrew 'who is like God'*.
Mildred	brings forth awareness of the ascending light creating radiance and echoing creation. *Old English 'mild and counsel'*.
Moira	brings forth in childlike innocence awareness of the radiating light purified. *Celtic 'soft'*.
Molly	brings forth in childlike innocence two ways of ascending light in awareness. *Version of Mary*.
Monica	is bringing forth in childlike innocence of the self awareness of beauty purified. *Greek 'alone'*.
Morag	brings forth in childlike innocence radiance purifying goodness. *Gaelic 'great'*.
Muriel	brings forth and carries radiance of awareness which reflects the ascending light. *Old Irish 'sea bright'*.
Myra	brings forth awareness of radiance purified. *Origin unknown*.
Nadine	is the self purifying creation in awareness of the self reflected. *Russian 'hope'*.
Nancy	is the self purifying the self in beauty of awareness. *Pet form of Ann*.

Neil	is the self reflecting awareness of the ascending light. *Irish 'a champion'*.
Nicholas	is the self in awareness of beauty rising up God's stepladder in childlike innocence of the ascending light purifying one half of eternity. *Greek 'victory and people'*.
Nicola	is the self being aware of beauty and the childlike innocence of the ascending light purified. *Fem. form of Nicholas*.
Nigel	is the self being aware of goodness and reflecting the ascending light. *Latin 'somewhat black'*.
Nora	is the self in childlike innocence radiating purity. *Form of Eleanor*.
Norma	is the self in childlike innocence and radiance bringing forth purity. *Latin 'rule'*.
Norman	is the self in childlike innocence and radiance bringing forth purity of the self. *Old English 'a northman'*.
Olga	is the childlike innocence of the ascending light of goodness purified. *Scandinavian 'inviolable, holy'*.
Olive	is childlike innocence in the ascending light and awareness of the descending light which is reflected. *From the tree*.
Oliver	is childlike innocence in the ascending light and awareness of the descending light which reflects radiating light. *Masc. form of Olive*.
Oscar	is the childlike innocence of one half of eternity and the beauty of the purity of radiance. *Gaelic 'God and spear'*.
Oswald	is childlike innocence of one half of eternity, and two ways of descending light which purify the ascending light of creation. *Old English 'God and power'*.

Paddy   is the heart centre purifying creation and creating awareness. *Pet form of Patrick.*

Pamela   is the heart purifying the bringing forth of reflections of the ascending light purified. *From Sir Philip Sidney's poem 'Arcadia' (1590).*

Pat   is the heart purified by time. *Pet form of Patrick or Patricia.*

Patricia   is the heart purifying time and radiating awareness of beauty in awareness of purity. *Fem. form of Patrick.*

Patrick   is the heart purifying time and radiating awareness of beauty and planting it in God's planting field. *Latin 'a nobleman'; apostle of the Irish.*

Patsy   is the heart purified by time in one half of eternity and awareness of it. *Version of Patricia.*

Paul   is the heart which purifies and carries the ascending light. *Latin 'small'.*

Pauline   is the heart which purifies and carries the ascending light in awareness of the self reflected. *Fem. form of Paul.*

Pearl   is the heart reflecting purity in the radiance of the ascending light. *Jewel name.*

Penelope   is the heart mirroring the self, reflecting the ascending light in childlike innocence of the heart reflected. *Greek 'thread on the bobbin in the shuttle'.*

Percy   is the heart reflecting the radiating light in the beauty of awareness. *Surname, place name.*

Peter   is the heart reflecting time and mirroring the radiating light. *Greek 'stone'.*

Philip   is the heart rising up God's stepladder in awareness of the radiating light and awareness of the heart centre. *Greek 'fond of horses'.*

Philomena   is the heart rising up God's stepladder in awareness of the ascending light and in childlike innocence, bringing forth reflections of the self purified. *Greek 'I am loved'*.

Phyllis   is the heart rising up God's stepladder in awareness of two ways of ascending light and awareness of one half of eternity. *Greek 'leafy'*.

Polly   is the heart of innocence and awareness of two ways of ascending light. *Pet form of Mary*.

Poppy   is the heart of innocence and the heart centre of awareness. *Flower name*.

Primrose   is the heart radiating awareness and bringing forth and radiating childlike innocence of one half of eternity which is reflected. *Flower name*.

Quentin   is the initiation of carrying awareness of the self and through time awareness of the self. *Latin 'the fifth'*.

Rachel   is radiating the purity of beauty up God's stepladder and reflecting the ascending light. *Hebrew 'a ewe'*.

Ralph   is radiating the purity of the ascending light of the heart up God's stepladder to beyond the beyond. *Old English 'counsel and wolf'*.

Raymond   is radiating the purity of awareness and bringing forth childlike innocence of the self in creativity. *Germanic 'advice and defence'*.

Rebecca   is radiating reflected light along the sacred path, reflecting beauty and beautifying purity. *Hebrew 'a heifer'*.

Reginald   is radiance reflecting goodness in awareness of the self and purifying the ascending light of creation. *Germanic 'mighty and sway'*.

Reuben   is the radiance which is reflected and carried along the sacred path, reflecting the self. *Hebrew 'behold a son'*.

Rhoda   is radiating the light up God's stepladder in childlike innocence and creating purity. *Greek 'rose'*.

Richard   is radiating awareness of beauty, rising up God's stepladder and purifying the radiance of creation. *Germanic 'ruler and hard'*.

Robert   is the radiance of childlike innocence along the Divine path echoing the radiance of crystallized light. *Germanic 'fame and bright'*.

Robin   is the radiance of childlike innocence along the sacred path of awareness of the self. *Pet form of Robert*.

Roderick   is the radiance of childlike innocence of creation, mirrored in the radiating light in awareness of the beauty which is being planted. *Germanic 'fame and rule'*.

Roger   is the radiance of the childlike innocence of God, reflected in the radiating light. *O'd High German 'fame and spear'*.

Roland   is radiating the light of childlike innocence through the ascending light of purity of the self in creativity. *Germanic 'fame and land'*.

Rona   is radiating childlike innocence of the self purified. *Fem. form of Ronald*.

Ronald   is radiating the light of childlike innocence of the self and purifying the ascending light of creation. *Version of Reginald*.

Rory   is radiating the light of innocence and radiating the light of awareness. *Celtic 'red'*.

Rosalind   is radiating childlike innocence of one half of eternity and purifying the ascending light in awareness of the self in creativity. *Old German 'horse-serpent'.*

Rosamund is radiating childlike innocence of one half of eternity in purity and bringing forth and carrying the self in creativity. *Germanic 'protection'.*

Rose is the radiance of the childlike innocence of one half of eternity and the reflections of it. *Flower name.*

Ross is the radiance of the childlike innocence of the two halves of eternity. *Surname.*

Roy is radiating the light of childlike innocence and awareness. *Old French 'king'.*

Rupert is radiating and carrying the light of the heart and reflecting and radiating time. *Version of Robert.*

Russell is the radiance of carrying for two halves of eternity and reflecting two ways of ascending light. *Old French 'redhead'.*

Ruth is radiance which carries time up God's stepladder to beyond the beyond. *Biblical name.*

Ryan is radiating awareness and purity of the self. *Irish surname.*

Sabrina is one half of eternity purifying the sacred path which is lit by the radiating light in awareness of the self purified. *Early name of River Severn.*

Samantha is one half of eternity purified, bringing forth purity of the self through time up God's stepladder in purity. *Fem. form of Samuel.*

Samuel is one half of eternity purified, bringing forth and carrying reflections of the ascending light. *Hebrew 'Shem is God'.*

Sandra is one half of eternity purifying the self and creating and radiating purity. *Pet form of Alexandra.*

Sarah is one half of eternity purifying and radiating the purity of rising up God's stepladder to beyond the beyond.*Hebrew 'princess'.*

Scott is one half of eternity beautifying in childlike innocence the essence of time twice over. *Surname.*

Sean is one half of eternity reflecting and purifying the self. *Irish form of John.*

Selina is one half of eternity reflecting the ascending light in awareness of the self purified. *Latin 'heaven'.*

Sharon is one half of eternity rising up God's stepladder purifying and radiating innocence of the self. *Palestine place name.*

Sheena is one half of eternity rising up God's stepladder echoing and reflecting the self purified. *Scottish form of Jean.*

Sheila is one half of eternity rising up God's stepladder reflecting awareness of the ascending light purified. *Irish form of Cecilia.*

Shirley is one half of eternity rising up the heavenly steps in awareness, radiating the ascending light and reflecting awareness. *Surname.*

Shona is one half of eternity rising up God's stepladder in childlike innocence of the self purified. *Fem. form of John.*

Simon is one half of eternity in awareness of bringing forth childlike innocence of the self. *Hebrew 'God has heard'.*

Sonia is one half of eternity in childlike innocence of the self and awareness of purity. *From Sophia.*

Sophia is one half of eternity in childlike innocence of the heart rising up God's stepladder in the awareness of purity. *Greek meaning 'wisdom'*.

Sophie is one half of eternity in childlike innocence of the heart rising up God's stepladder in the awareness of reflection. *From Sophia*.

Stacey is one half of eternity in time of purity and beauty reflecting awareness. *Form of Anastasia*.

Stanley is one half of eternity in time of purity of the self and the ascending light reflected in awareness. *Surname, place name; Old English 'stony meadow'*.

Stella is one half of eternity in time of reflection of two ways of ascending light purified. *Latin 'a star'*.

Stephanie is one half of eternity in time of reflection of the heart rising up God's stepladder in purity of the self and in awareness of reflected light. *Fem. form of Stephen*.

Stephen is one half of eternity in time of reflection of the heart rising up God's stepladder reflecting the self. *Greek 'a garland'*.

Steven is one half of eternity in time of reflection of the descending light mirrored in the self. *Version of Stephen*.

Stuart is one half of eternity in time of carrying the purity of the radiance of crystallized light. *Scottish clan name*.

Susan is one half of eternity carrying and one half of eternity purifying the self. *Hebrew 'lily'*.

Swein is one half of eternity and two ways of descending light which reflect awareness of the self. *Viking name*.

Sydney is one half of eternity being aware of creation of the self in the echoes of awareness. *Surname, place name*.

Sylvia   is one half of eternity being aware of the ascending light and the descending light in awareness of purity. *Latin 'wood'.*

Tabitha   is a time of purity and the heavenly path of awareness of time rising up God's step-ladder in purity. *Aramaic 'gazelle'.*

Terence   is the time of reflection radiating the light of echoes of the self and beauty which is mirrored. *Roman poet's name.*

Teresa   is the time of reflection of the radiating light which reflects one half of eternity purified. *Latin, meaning uncertain.*

Thomas   is the time of rising up God's stepladder in childlike innocence and bringing forth the purity of one half of eternity. *Aramaic 'a twin'.*

Thora   is the time of rising up God's stepladder in childlike innocence and radiating the light of purity. *Fem. form of Norse god Thor.*

Timothy   is the time of awareness bringing forth childlike innocence and the time of rising up God's stepladder in awareness. *Greek 'honour and God'.*

Tina   is the time of awareness of the self purified. *Pet form of Christina.*

Toby   is the time of innocence on the path to awareness. *Hebrew 'Jehovah is good'.*

Tracy   is time radiating the purity of the beauty of awareness. *English form of Teresa.*

Trevor   is the time of radiance, reflecting the descending light in childlike innocence and radiance. *Surname.*

Una   is the carrying of the self purified. *Irish name.*

Ursula is carrying the radiance of one half of eternity and carrying the ascending light of creation. *Latin 'she-bear'*.

Valda is the descending light purified and the ascending light of creation purified. *Origin unknown*.

Valerie is the descending light purified and the ascending light reflecting and radiating awareness in reflection. *Latin 'to be strong'*.

Vanessa is the descending light of purity of the self reflecting two halves of eternity purified. *Fictional name*.

Vera is the descending light reflecting and radiating purity. *Latin 'truth'*.

Veronica is the descending light reflecting and radiating childlike innocence of the self in awareness of beauty which is purified. *Biblical name*.

Victor is the descending light of awareness beautifying time in the childlike innocence of radiance. *Latin 'conqueror'*.

Victoria is the descending light of awareness of beauty in a time of childlike innocence of radiance and awareness of purity. *Fem. form of Victor*.

Vincent is the descending light of awareness of the self, and beauty of reflections of the self in crystallized light. *Latin 'conquering'*.

Violet is the descending light of awareness in childlike innocence of the ascending light reflecting time. *Flower name*.

Virginia is the descending light of awareness of the radiance of goodness in awareness of the self and awareness of purity. *Latin 'a maiden'*.

Vivien is the descending light of awareness twice over reflecting the self. *Latin 'alive'*.

Walter   is two ways of descending light purifying the ascending light in time of reflection of radiance. *Old High German 'sway and army'.*

Wanda   is two ways of descending light purifying the self and creating purity. *German name.*

Wendy   is two ways of descending light reflecting the self and creating awareness. *Fictional name (Peter Pan).*

Wilfred   is two ways of descending light being aware of the ascending light and faith in the radiance of reflections of creation. *Old English 'will and peace, protection'.*

William   is two ways of descending light being aware of two ways of ascending light and awareness of the purity of manifestation. *Old High German 'will, resolution and helmet'.*

Wilma   is two ways of descending light being aware of the ascending light which is bringing forth purity. *Fem. form of William.*

Winifred   is two ways of descending light being aware of the self and awareness of faith in the radiance of reflections of creation. *Welsh 'blessed reconciliation'.*

Yvonne   is awareness of the descending light, child-like innocence of the self and the self in reflection. *French name.*

Zoe   is the heavenly and earthly planes innocently reflecting themselves. *Greek 'life'.*

Endword

IN YOUR ATTEMPTS TO find your inner sacredness remember that ultimately your personal goal is to find that which is good, noble and of the most beautiful in your life. Start thinking of your inner life as God's living light and that you are a walking storage house of loving light. Steadfastly continue to search for God's sacred lamp of wisdom. Continue to sing and dance for the trees, birds, plants, animals and places and things for we are all one in the life of the omnipresence.

It is true that we choose to develop and grow by our experience. Sometimes this involves trial and error which can be painful at times because we are the give-away. When we give ourselves totally and completely to life, we immediately create the power for our own personal transcendence in that single action. And as soon as we take an action which takes away from life we in turn give away to life something of ourselves. It is only in giving that we receive.

Appendix 1: Everyday Words as Metaphors

Dictionary definition	Metaphor
ACORN *Noun*: the fruit of an oak tree.	*Acorn* is purity that purifies the beauty of the childlike innocence that radiates onto the self.
ACOUSTICS The study of sound. The characteristics (of a hall, etc.) which affect the hearing of sound in it.	*Acoustics* is a purity that purifies the beauty of childlike innocence as in the lifting from the floor of the Earth to the Heavens; allowing time to crystallize into awareness, so that its beauty can become the other side of eternity.
ACQUAINT *Verb*: to make (someone) familiar (with).	*Acquaint* is purity that purifies the beauty of the eternal quest thereby lifting purification as awareness in the infinite self through time.
BELOW *Prep*: lower in position.	*Below* is the sacred path of our relations as we travel to the heavens in childlike innocence inside the essence of descending light.

BELT   *Noun*: a band or strip of leather, cloth, etc. worn around the waist.

Belt is the path of the reflective universe as it travels in ascending light in relationship with time.

BENCH   *Noun*: a long seat; a work-table; the judges of a court.

Bench is the path of the reflective universe as it integrates the infinite and finite of the self as beauty then moves it along the rungs of the stepladder unto the greater mystery.

CASH   *Noun*: money in the form of coins and notes.

Cash is beauty that purifies itself beyond one half of eternity just before it climbs beyond the beyond.

CASHEW   *Noun*: a type of kidney-shaped nut, or the large tropical tree that bears it.

Cashew is beauty that purifies itself beyond one half of eternity just before it climbs beyond the beyond, and then through the reflective universe can see itself by way of descending light.

CASHMERE   *Noun*: fine soft goat's wool.

Cashmere is beauty that purifies itself beyond one half of eternity just before it climbs beyond the beyond and then materialism becomes the reflection and its radiance mirrors back to it what it sees.

DIE   *Verb*: to lose life: to wither.

Die is the throwing light of awareness transformed beyond reflectivity.

DIET   *Noun*: food.

Diet is the throwing light of awareness transformed beyond reflectivity so that it can become the equidistant cross balance.

DIFFER   *Verb*: to disagree.

Differ is the throwing light of awareness from which faith illuminates and thereby changes reflectivity into divine radiance.

ECHO   *Noun*: the repeating of a sound caused by striking a surface and coming back.

Echo is the reflectivity that in its most divine beauty chooses to climb God's stepladder in order to go beyond its own divine innocence.

ECLIPSE   *Noun*: the disappearance of the whole or part of a heavenly body, as of the sun when the moon comes between it and the earth.

Eclipse is the reflectivity of beauty that transfers awareness to the heart of the circle of light and then produces the other half of eternity into the echoes of all our relations.

ECOLOGY   *Noun*: the study of plants, animals, etc. in relation to their natural surroundings.

Ecology is reflectivity, beauty, innocence and the ascending light that transforms the innocence in goodness so that matter can have living awareness.

FINITE   *Adj*: having an end or limit.

Finite is the faith in awareness of the planetary self that brings awareness through crystallized light onto resonance and then assumes its posture.

FIR   *Noun*: a kind of cone-bearing tree.

Fir is the radiance found inside awareness.

FIRE   *Noun*: the heat and light given off by something burning.

Fire is faith in the root of the eternal flame of life that changes awareness into radiance just before it becomes the reflective universe.

GENERATE   *Verb*: to produce, bring into being.

Generate is the goodness of reflectivity that is found in the self, the reflectivity of radiance that is purifying itself in time.

GENEROUS   *Adj*: giving plentifully, kind.

Generous is the goodness in the personal self that places the radiance of innocence thereby lifting the down below into the up above.

GENESIS   *Noun*: beginning.

Genesis is the goodness of reflectivity that is found in the self and is the reflectivity of awareness of the upper and lower planes.

HORSE   *Noun*: a type of four-footed animal with hooves and a mane.

Horse is the stepladder to the heavens beyond innocence radiating one half of eternity as a reflection.

HORTICULTURE   *Noun*: the study and art of gardening.

Horticulture is rising up God's stepladder in childlike innocence radiating the awareness of time, carrying beauty through the ascending light and through time carrying the radiating light that reflects itself.

HOSANNA   *Noun*: an exclamation of praise to God.

Hosanna is the stepladder to the heavenly planes in childlike innocence of one half of eternity that is purifying the personal self so that the infinite self may be pure.

INCAPABLE   *Adj*: unable (to do what is expected).

Incapable is awareness in the self as the beauty of the purifying heart; of the purity of the path of the connection of the ascending light as in its own reflection.

INCARCERATE *Verb*: to imprison.

Incarcerate is the awareness of the self; of the beauty of purity of its radiance of abundance; of the beauty of a mirrored reflection radiating purity through time reflected.

INCENSE *Noun*: spices burned (specially in religious ceremonies) to give off a pleasant smell.

Incense is the awareness of the self; of the beauty of the reflectivity of the self as in the other side of eternity as it reflects upon its own beingness.

JOINT *Noun*: a place where two or more things join.

Joint is the eyes through which innocence sees the awareness of the self by way of crystallized time.

JOKE *Noun*: anything said or done to cause laughter.

Joke is seeing childlike innocence that is planting reflectivity.

JOURNEY *Noun*: a distance travelled.

Journey is the vision of childlike innocence carrying the radiating light beyond the self so that the mirrored reflection of awareness can be made.

KNACK *Noun*: a special clever ability.

Knack is the planting field of the infinite self as it purifies the beauty of the sowing art.

KNAPSACK *Noun*: a bag for food, clothes, etc. slung on the back.

Knapsack is planting the self in the awareness of the heart of one half of eternity as in the purifying beauty of God's planting fields.

KNEAD   *Verb*: to work (dough, etc.) by pressing with the fingers: to massage.

Knead is to plant the infinite self into reflectivity of awareness through the action of doing.

LEPRECHAUN   *Noun*: a kind of Irish fairy.

Leprechaun is the ascending light of reflectivity of the heart, radiating, echoing beauty of the stepladder to the heavens, purifying and carrying the Divine self.

LILY   *Noun*: a tall plant grown from a bulb with large white or coloured flowers.

Lily is the ascending light of awareness.

LOAF   *Noun*: a shaped mass of bread.

Loaf is the ascending light of innocence purified into faith.

LOCH   *Noun*: (in Scotland) a lake, an arm of the sea.

Loch is the ascending light of childlike innocence beautified and rising up God's stepladder to the heavenly planes.

LOG   *Noun*: a thick rough piece of wood.

Log is the ascending light of childlike innocence and goodness.

LYNX   *Noun*: a kind of wild animal.

Lynx is the ascending light of awareness of the self empowered.

MATE   *Noun*: a companion or fellow worker.

Mate is matter that is purifying itself through time by way of reflection.

MATERIAL   *Adj*: made of matter, able to be seen and felt.

Material is bringing forth purification of time by way of reflection so that it may radiate the abundance of awareness of the purifying light of the ascending light.

MATERNAL   *Adj*: of a mother, like a mother.

Maternal is matter of purifyingness of time of reflectivity of radiance of the self beyond the purity of the ascending light.

NEAR   *Adj*: not far away in place or time; close in relationship, friendship, etc.

Near is the infinite self echoing purity of the radiating light.

NECK   *Noun*: the part between the head and the body.

Neck is the self reflecting beauty of the essence of planting.

NEED   *Verb*: to be without, to be in want of, to require.

Need is the infinite self reflecting twice over the mirroring of its creation.

OATH   *Noun*: a solemn promise to speak the truth, to keep one's word, to be loyal, etc.

Oath is innocence purifying time up the stepladder.

OBSERVE   *Verb*: to notice, to watch with attention, to remark, to obey (a law, etc.) to keep, preserve.

Observe is childlike innocence that is bringing one half of eternity into the reflectivity by bringing down the light and reflecting it through radiance.

OBTAIN   *Verb*: to get, gain.

Obtain is childlike innocence that is bringing time into awareness and purifying the self.

PACEMAKER   *Noun*: a person who sets the pace (as in a race), a device used to correct weak or irregular heart rhythms.

Pacemaker is the heart purifying beauty through reflectivity while manifesting and washing God's planting field and reflecting it through radiance.

PAD   *Noun*: a soft cushion-like object to prevent jarring or rubbing.

Pad is the heart purifying creation.

PAGAN *Noun*: a person who does not believe in any religion: a heathen.

Pagan is God's heart that is purifying goodness before it purifies itself.

QUARTET *Noun*: a group of four players or singers, a piece of music written for such a group.

Quartet is the initiation that carries the purifying radiance through time and reflects it through crystallized thought.

QUARTZ *Noun*: a kind of hard substance often in crystal form, found in rocks.

Quartz is the initiation that carries the purifying radiance through time as above so below.

QUASAR *Noun*: a star-like object (not really a star) which gives out light and radar waves.

Quasar is initiation that carries and purifies the other side of eternity and purifies the radiating light.

RAINBOW *Noun*: the brilliant coloured bow or arch sometimes to be seen in the sky opposite the sun when rain is falling.

Rainbow is the radiating light of purity of awareness of the self, while bringing childlike innocence and carrying it not once but twice over.

RAISE *Verb*: to lift up, raise the flag, to cause to rise, make higher.

Raise is the radiating light purifying awareness of one half of eternity with reflectivity.

RAKE *Noun*: a tool like a large comb with a long handle, for smoothing earth, gathering hay, etc.

Rake is the radiating light purifying planting the echoes of itself.

SACRED *Adj*: Holy, devoted to or dedicated to some purpose or person, sacred to her memory, connected with religion.

Sacred is one half of eternity that is purifying beauty and radiating the reflection of creation.

SACRIFICE   *Noun*: the act of offering something (such as an animal that has been specially killed) to a god, something given up in order to benefit another person.

Sacrifice is one half of eternity that is purifying beauty and radiating awareness through faith so that awareness can become beauty through reflectivity.

SADDLE   *Noun*: a seat for a rider used on the back of a horse or on a bicycle, etc.

Saddle is one half of eternity that is purifying the action of doing not once but twice of the ascending light of reflectivity.

TADPOLE   *Noun*: a young frog or toad in its first stage of life.

Tadpole is time that is purifying the action of doing through God's heart so that innocence may ascend as reflectivity.

TAKE   *Verb*: to lay hold of, to grasp.

Take is time purifying the planting of the soul with reflectivity.

TALE   *Noun*: a story of real or imaginary events.

Tale is time purifying the ascending light and reflecting it.

ULTIMATE   *Adj*: last, final.

Ultimate is carrying the ascending light through time allowing awareness to permeate creativity while purifying the echoes of reflectivity.

UMBRELLA   *Noun*: an object made up of a folding covered framework on a stick which protects against rain.

Umbrella is carrying matter along the sacred path in the radiating light of reflectivity while allowing the ascending light of purity.

UMPIRE *Noun*: (in cricket, tennis) a person who sees that the game is played according to the rules and decides doubtful points, a judge who is asked to settle a dispute.

Umpire is carrying the light of bringing forth from the heart of awareness while radiating the reflectivity of Divine placement.

VALOUR *Noun*: courage, bravery.

Valour is the descending light purifying its self and the ascending light of childlike innocence carrying radiance.

VANGUARD *Noun*: the part of an army going in front of the main body, the leading group in a movement, etc.

Vanguard is the descending light of purity of the Divine self: of goodness carrying purity while radiating the action of doingness.

VANISH *Verb*: to go out of sight, to fade away to nothing.

Vanish is the descending light purifying the self with awareness of one half of eternity beyond the stepladder.

WARN *Verb*: to tell (a person) beforehand about possible danger, misfortune, etc.

Warn is the essence that carries not once but twice over the purity of the radiating light of the infinite self.

WASH *Verb*: to clean with water, soap, etc.

Wash is the carrying light that carries all of life not just once but twice over while purifying the other side of eternity up the stepladder into the heavens.

WASP *Noun*: a stinging winged type of insect, with a slender yellow and black striped body.

Wasp is the carrying light that carries life not once but twice over while purifying the other side of eternity with the heart.

XMAS *Noun*: short for Christmas.

Xmas is power of the manifesting light bringing purity to one half of eternity.

X-RAYS *Noun*: plural – rays that can pass through many substances impossible for light to pass through, and produce, on photographic film, a shadow picture (called an X-ray) of the object through which they have passed.

X-rays are powers of radiating light of purity bringing awareness of one half of eternity.

YACHT *Noun*: a sailing or motor-driven vessel for racing, cruising, etc.

Yacht is awareness purifying beauty up the stepladder into time.

YARROW *Noun*: a strong smelling type of plant with flat clusters of white flowers.

Yarrow is awareness radiating light not once but twice into innocence while carrying its own divinity.

YEAR *Noun*: the time taken by the earth to go once round the sun, about 365 days: the period 1st January to 31st December, or a period of twelve months starting at any point.

Year is awareness reflecting purity by way of radiating light.

ZEAL *Noun*: enthusiasm, keenness, determination.

Zeal is heaven and earth reflecting purity of the ascending light.

ZENITH *Noun*: point of the heavens which is exactly overhead; the highest point (of achievement, etc.).

Zenith is the heavenly and earthly planes placing the self into awareness by way of time just before climbing the stepladder into the upper realms.

ZERO *Noun*: nothing or the sign for it (0).

Zero is the heavenly and earthly planes seeking the placement of the radiating light through childlike innocence.

Appendix 2: Gemstones as Metaphors

GEMS   are goodness reflecting the bringing forth of one
          half of the other side of eternity.

ABALONE   is the washing light bringing purity of the
          ascending light and innocence of the infinite self
          through reflection.

AMBER   is the purifying of materialism bringing reflec-
          tions of the radiating light.

AMETHYST is the purifying light of materialism reflecting
          crystallized thought up the stepladder of aware-
          ness of the other side of eternity inside time.

CITRINE   is beauty of awareness in time; of radiating light
          of awareness; of the self; of reflectivity.

CORAL   is the beauty of innocence radiating purity of the
          ascending light.

DIAMOND   is the action of awareness purifying materialism;
          of childlike innocence of the self; of the action of
          doingness.

EMERALD   is the placement of materialism affecting the
          radiating light of purification of the ascending
          light of creation.

GARNET — is goodness of purity of the self of reflectivity within crystallized thoughts.

JADE — is the seeing eyes of purity through the action of creating reflection.

MOONSTONE — is bringing forth innocence and through innocence of the infinite self in one half of eternity and crystallizing the light of innocence of the self in reflection.

ONYX — is the childlike innocence of the self of awareness empowered.

OPAL — is the childlike innocence of the heart purifying the ascending light.

PEARL — is the heart reflecting purity radiating the ascending light.

RUBY — is the radiating light carrying the sacred path of awareness.

SAPPHIRE — is half of eternity purifying God's heart twice over and the stepladder of awareness radiating reflection.

TOPAZ — is the time of innocence of the heart purifying the as above so below.

TURQUOISE — is of time carrying the radiating light of initiation, of carrying innocence of awareness, of one half of eternity in reflectivity.

Glossary

Awareness	Awareness is to be fully awake with the inspirational zeal of inner meaning.
Breath	The breath is the inspirational emanations of the inner source.
Carrying	Carrying is the omnipresence of the Tao which carries all life.
Chant	Chant is the metaphor for creating the openings needed to plug into the here and now orientation.
Childlike innocence	is to be an open channel with no obstructions or hindrances.
Circle	The circle or medicine wheel is the symbolic form for the seed of constant changes that are continually manifesting as new life that is in the state of germination into spiritual as well as into natural law.
Dance	Dance is the physical process for the expansion of personal, planetary and cosmic awareness.
Doing	Doing is the art of giving personally or cosmically.
Essence	The essence is the walk and the talk of the Divine presence in all created formulas.

Evolution	is to ascend.
Fasting	is the process by which the outer self dies into the inner truth.
Give-away	is the same as the action that takes place when one ascends to a higher level in consciousness.
Innocence	Only in the innocence of a child can one enter beyond the gates to the truth of Godliness.
Insight	The insights are the connections to the inspirational gifts of the metaphoric mind.
Language	is the movement of energy.
Laughter	is the spirit of making and building God's presence.
Materialism	is matter creating the goals and objectives of the infinite self.
Medicine wheel	is the ever-unfolding seed of life.
Metaphor	The metaphor expresses the Divine presence within the context of a personal experience.
Mouth	is to see and be greatness so that as the sound passes through it it endows the sounds with its essence.
Movement	is beauty unfolding; it is also life either in states of growth or decay.
Music	Music is seeing the truth through the eyes of the perceptual being.
Name	In metaphor, the name of a human person will be centred in its resonance to the physical lungs of the person carrying a specific name.
Name giver	is the lungs of the Creator.
People	The people are the vibrations that contain life at all levels.

Placement Placement is God sitting and waiting for us to travel between two slices of light into the cosmic heart on our return home to the infinite.

Principle ideas The principle ideas are the main forms from which other related ideas emerge.

Purification Purification is washing the impurities out of the mental, emotional, physical and spiritual bodies.

Qualitative is the spirit that lives in all forms.

Radiance is the polarity of the struggles that are necessary for movement to take place.

Resonance is the ever-unfolding of life.

Sound Sound is listening and worshipping of the materialization of matter through movement.

Streams The streams connect consciousness to memory.

Tracks of dancing light are all the people who came in the past and all those in the future. People who will walk their talk for a while on their earthly journey and then, having completed it, will return home, leaving only their tracks so that all future generations may be guided in their dance by the tracks of dancing light.

Use The word use means to be open to the inner voice because to use or employ a process is to create a link with the inner spiritual guidance necessary for learning.

Vibration The people and vibration refer to the resonance of the living vibrance in all things Godly.